Congressional
Research Service

Informing the legislative debate since 1914 _____

Gulf Coast Restoration: RESTORE Act and Related Efforts

Charles V. Stern
Specialist in Natural Resources Policy

Pervaze A. Sheikh
Specialist in Natural Resources Policy

Jonathan L. Ramseur
Specialist in Environmental Policy

January 27, 2014

Congressional Research Service

7-5700

www.crs.gov

R43380

Summary

The Gulf of Mexico coastal environment (Gulf Coast) stretches over approximately 600,000 square miles across five U.S. states: Texas, Louisiana, Mississippi, Alabama, and Florida. It is home to more than 22 million people and more than 15,000 species of sea life. This environment has been degraded over time due to, among other things, altered hydrology, loss of barrier islands and coastal wetland habitat, issues associated with low water quality, and other human impacts and natural processes. Pre-existing environmental issues throughout the Gulf Coast have been affected and in some cases exacerbated by recent natural hazards and manmade catastrophes. Among other events, Hurricanes Katrina and Rita caused widespread damage to wetland and coastal areas along the Gulf.

A number of federal efforts are ongoing to restore parts of the Gulf Coast, including major projects by the Army Corps of Engineers, the Fish and Wildlife Service, the National Oceanic and Atmospheric Administration, and the Environmental Protection Agency, among other federal agencies. Significant state and local efforts to restore the Gulf Coast have also been undertaken, in some cases in consultation with the federal government.

The *Deepwater Horizon* explosion on April 20, 2010, resulted in an unprecedented discharge of oil in U.S. waters, and eventually resulted in the oiling of over 1,100 miles of shoreline. As an identified responsible party, BP is liable for response (i.e., cleanup) costs, as well as specified economic damages and natural resource damages related to the spill. As of the date of this report, oil cleanup operations continue, as well as various claims processes that seek to compensate parties for damages related to the spill.

Efforts to mitigate and recover from damages associated from the *Deepwater Horizon* spill have initiated several new processes that are expected to supplement ongoing Gulf Coast restoration work. In particular, three major processes are likely to significantly affect restoration work going forward: first, the dissemination of Clean Water Act penalties through the Gulf Coast Ecosystem Restoration Trust Fund, as required by Congress in the RESTORE Act (P.L. 112-141); second, the dissemination of $2.55 billion in criminal penalties from responsible parties by the National Fish and Wildlife Foundation, as required under relevant court settlements; and third, the assessment and provision of Natural Resources Damage Assessment (NRDA) Penalties under the Oil Pollution Act of 1990, as amended (P.L. 101-380).

Congressional interest in these efforts may include oversight of previously passed legislation (P.L. 112-141 and P.L. 101-380) and any related changes. Congress may also be interested in the effect of these efforts on ongoing Gulf Coast restoration efforts, coordination between the multiple aforementioned processes, and the effectiveness of these efforts going forward.

Contents

Figures

Tables

Appendixes

Contacts

Introduction

The Gulf of Mexico coastal region (Gulf Coast) stretches over the shoreline areas of five U.S. states: Texas, Louisiana, Mississippi, Alabama, and Florida. The coastal environment has been altered over time due to changes in hydrology, loss of barrier islands and coastal wetland habitat, issues associated with low water quality, human development, and natural processes, among other things. The federal government has addressed these changes through ecosystem restoration activities in the region over the past few decades. Major restoration projects led by the U.S. Army Corps of Engineers (Corps), the Fish and Wildlife Service (FWS), the National Oceanic and Atmospheric Administration (NOAA), and the Environmental Protection Agency (EPA) have been implemented. Significant state and local efforts to restore the Gulf Coast have also been undertaken, in some cases in consultation with the federal government.

The Gulf Coast has also been affected by large-scale natural and manmade disasters that have significantly affected the environment and economic vitality of the region. Indeed, these disasters have also led to changes in restoration efforts, sometimes in a significant fashion. For example, in 2005, Hurricanes Katrina and Rita caused widespread damage to wetland and coastal areas along the Gulf, and altered the plans for restoring some parts of the coast. In 2010, a manmade disaster, the *Deepwater Horizon* oil spill, resulted in an unprecedented discharge of oil in U.S. waters and oiling of over 1,100 miles of shoreline.[1] The oil spill had short-term ecological effects on coastal habitats and species, and is expected to result in long-term ecological effects (these effects are largely uncertain). This event increased attention towards the Gulf Coast environment and modified perceptions about restoring the Gulf Coast ecosystem. In particular, the oil spill focused attention on the natural resources impacted by the incident and long-term natural resource restoration issues that existed before the spill.

As an identified responsible party,[2] BP is liable for response (i.e., cleanup) costs, as well as specified economic and natural resource damages related to the spill.[3] As of the date of this report, oil cleanup operations were ongoing, as were various claims processes seeking to compensate parties for damages related to the spill. Some funds have already been released and targeted toward environmental and economic restoration. Some of the primary funding streams include:

- Clean Water Act (CWA) civil damages paid by responsible parties, 80% of which are expected to support the efforts outlined under the Resources and Ecosystems, Sustainability, Tourist Opportunities, and Revived Economies act of the Gulf Coast States Act of 2012 (Subtitle F of P.L. 112-141, also known as the RESTORE Act);

---

[1] See CRS Report R42942, *Deepwater Horizon Oil Spill: Recent Activities and Ongoing Developments*, by Jonathan L. Ramseur and Curry L. Hagerty, footnote 5.

[2] For the purpose of this report, BP is discussed as if it is the sole responsible party—a key term in the existing liability and compensation framework. However, other parties are also considered responsible parties. The Department of Justice named nine defendants in a civil suit filed December 15, 2010. See press release at http://www.justice.gov/opa/pr/2010/December/10-ag-1442.html.

[3] Oil Pollution Act, 33 U.S.C. §2702.

- other CWA civil and criminal penalties, including funding for projects to be selected by the National Fish and Wildlife Foundation (NFWF) under court settlements; and

- funding to compensate for spill impacts through the Natural Resources Damage Assessment (NRDA) process, a component of oil spill liability pursuant to the Oil Pollution Act.[4]

Each of these funding streams is subject to its own conditions, priorities, and processes, and is expected to be overseen by different entities. In some cases, funds may be spent only on restoration of habitat damaged by the oil spill. In other cases, funds can address a wider range of issues, such as economic development.

Congress has varying degrees of oversight and control over the dissemination of funding to restore the Gulf Coast. The RESTORE Act, enacted in July 2012, established a framework for the dissemination of expected civil penalties under the Clean Water Act. In this act, to provide for long-term environmental and economic restoration of the region, Congress authorized the creation of a trust fund to collect monies derived from these penalties, established guidelines for allocating and awarding funds for ecosystem and economic restoration, and provided for monitoring and reporting on progress of restoration. Separately, Congress also has an interest in overseeing other ongoing restoration processes, including the NRDA process (implemented by NOAA, pursuant to the Oil Spill Pollution Act) and the allocation of restoration funds to NFWF, an independent nonprofit that was established and funded by Congress and is subject to congressional oversight. In addition to these funding streams, Congress also funds (through discretionary appropriations) and oversees multiple federal agencies conducting ongoing restoration actions in the Gulf region that are often related to, but in some cases undertaken apart from, activities initiated since the *Deepwater Horizon* spill.

Restoration of the Gulf Coast is complicated from a congressional perspective because multiple restoration processes are interrelated, but largely occur outside of the traditional appropriations process (including funds being used by nonfederal sources). With multiple sources of funding for ecosystem and economic restoration, Congress may be interested in how one or more restoration processes implement their activities, how they coordinate with each other, and how they are approaching and affecting the restoration of the Gulf Coast.

This report provides information on environmental damage and restoration activities related to the *Deepwater Horizon* spill. An overview of how the RESTORE Act is being implemented and a discussion of multiple funding sources and plans to recover and restore the Gulf Coast environment are discussed. Further, potential issues for Congress related to this restoration initiative are presented.

Background on the Gulf Coast Ecosystem

The Gulf Coast region is home to more than 22 million people and 15,000 species over five southern states: Texas, Louisiana, Mississippi, Alabama, and Florida. Animal, plant, and microbial populations depend on the Gulf's unique processes to survive. Overall, the Gulf Coast

---

[4] 33 U.S.C. 2701.

ecosystem includes multiple interconnected ecosystems spanning 600,000 square miles of shoreline of the Gulf of Mexico.[5] These ecosystems provide services that encompass aesthetic, economic, and environmental values for their residents. For instance, barrier islands and wetland complexes provide defense for coastal communities against hurricanes and coastal storms. They are habitat for a number of commercially and recreationally important species of fish, invertebrates, mammals, and birds, including many threatened and endangered species. These ecosystems also filter water, remove and trap contaminants, and store carbon, among other functions.

The *Deepwater Horizon* spill is one of several events and ongoing processes that have altered the Gulf Coast ecosystems over time. Prior to the spill, the ecosystems were undergoing large changes due to human development and natural processes. For example, large-scale sediment and habitat loss was occurring, in part, due to altered water flows from the Mississippi River; water pollution was being exacerbated by excess nutrients such as phosphorus and nitrogen; and waterways were being altered due to dredging and levee construction; among other things.[6] The spill did not change many of these processes but altered perspectives on how federal and state governments approach restoration.

Pre-Spill Federal Restoration Activities in the Gulf

Prior to the *Deepwater Horizon* oil spill, several federal agencies were involved in a number of efforts to restore and conserve ecosystems in the Gulf Coast region. These efforts ranged from large-scale restoration initiatives in particular ecosystems to grant programs and projects focusing on distinct restoration issues. For example, the Corps is involved in an initiative that aims to restore wetlands and reduce wetland loss in coastal Louisiana. The program, termed the Louisiana Coastal Area Program, is expected to entail approximately $1.5 billion for the construction of coastal restoration features that involve habitat restoration and dredging, among other things. The **Appendix** to this report outlines a number of the major ongoing federal restoration efforts and initiatives in the Gulf.[7] Several interagency forums coordinate federal stewardship efforts and collaborative planning for Gulf Coast projects, some in cooperation with state, nonprofit, and local entities.

Over the years, the Gulf Coast region has not been addressed comprehensively as an area for restoration. There has been no overarching restoration initiative addressing the region, possibly because of the size of the region and variability in its ecosystems and governing entities. Further, there has been no central entity or program responsible for planning or implementing restoration activities. Instead, responsibilities have varied by area, timing, and scope, with various combinations of federal, state, local, and nonprofit entities implementing (and in some cases directing) restoration. For instance, Louisiana and Mississippi have ongoing comprehensive restoration plans focused on Corps projects in specific ecosystems within the states. These are federal/state partnerships and differ in terms of how far projects have progressed. There are no

---

[5] These areas are affected by activities in the Gulf of Mexico Watershed, which extends approximately 1,000 miles upstream and drains 40% of the United States.

[6] This report provides only a brief background and discussion of pre-existing environmental issues in the Gulf Coast. These issues are discussed in more detail in *America's Gulf Coast: A Long Term Recovery Plan after the Deepwater Horizon Oil Spill*, September 2010, pp 24-29. Available at http://www.oilspillcommission.gov/sites/default/files/ documents/Mabus_Report.pdf. Hereinafter "Mabus Report."

[7] This list does not include state or locally based efforts and is not exhaustive.

comparable initiatives in the Gulf Coast regions of Texas, Alabama, and northern Florida, respectively.[8] In these areas, states, along with other entities, have initiated restoration efforts. Further complicating a comprehensive effort to restore the region is the complexity of ecological issues in the region and their connection to ecosystems outside of the region. For example, excess nutrients that cause hypoxia in the Gulf Coast area are attributed in part to agricultural runoff in the northern reaches of the Mississippi River. Addressing restoration in the Gulf Coast cuts across regions and ecosystems, as well as jurisdictions within the federal government.

Efforts at unifying federal agency actions and developing a process for restoring the Gulf Coast region were initiated by the Obama Administration before the *Deepwater Horizon* spill. The Administration created a Gulf Coast Ecosystem Restoration Working Group, which was tasked with developing a strategy for restoring the Gulf Coast region.[9] The strategy is termed the Roadmap for Restoring Ecosystem Resiliency and Sustainability in the Louisiana and Mississippi Coasts. The intent of the Roadmap is to guide near-term restoration actions to be undertaken by agencies within the working group, and facilitate the coordination of federal restoration and protection activities. However, the *Deepwater Horizon* spill and resulting damages and financial compensation from litigation altered the federal government's approach to restoration and coordination. Some of the new structures that have developed as a result are discussed below.

Deepwater Horizon Oil Spill: Environmental Impacts

The explosion of the *Deepwater Horizon* offshore drilling rig on April 20, 2010, which took place 41 miles southeast of the Louisiana coast, resulted in an estimated 171 million gallons (4.1 million barrels) of oil discharged into the Gulf of Mexico over 84 days.[10] An additional 35 million gallons of oil escaped the well, but did not enter the Gulf environment, because BP recovered this oil directly from the wellhead.[11] At the time these calculations were made (July 14, 2010), approximately 50% of the oil had evaporated, dissolved, or been effectively removed from the Gulf environment through human activities. However, a substantial portion—over 100 million gallons—remained, in some form, in the Gulf of Mexico. The fate of the remaining oil in the Gulf is uncertain and might never be determined conclusively. Multiple challenges hinder determination of the fate of the oil in the Gulf, and as time progresses, determining the fate of the oil and related environmental impacts will likely become more difficult. Some study results indicate that microbial organisms (bacteria) consumed and broke down a considerable amount of the oil in the water column.[12]

---

[8] There is, however, a comprehensive federal/state restoration plan for the Everglades (located in central and south Florida). For more information, see CRS Report R42007, *Everglades Restoration: Federal Funding and Implementation Progress*, by Charles V. Stern.

[9] A summary of these efforts is available at http://www.whitehouse.gov/administration/eop/ceq/initiatives/gulfcoast.

[10] See the Federal Interagency Solutions Group, Oil Budget Calculator Science and Engineering Team, Oil Budget Calculator: Deepwater Horizon-Technical Documentation, November 2010. See also CRS Report R41531, *Deepwater Horizon Oil Spill: The Fate of the Oil*, by Jonathan L. Ramseur.

[11] In February 2013, the federal government agreed with BP that this volume of oil would not be considered toward the CWA penalty determination. See United States District Court, Eastern District of Louisiana, Stipulation Mooting BP's Motion for Partial Summary Judgement, February 19, 2013, at http://www.laed.uscourts.gov/OilSpill/OilSpill htm.

[12] See, e.g., David Valentine et al, "Dynamic autoinoculation and the microbial ecology of a deep water hydrocarbon irruption," *Proceedings of the National Academy of Sciences*, January 2012; Bethanie Edwards et al., "Rapid Microbial Respiration of Oil from the Deepwater Horizon Spill in Offshore Surface Waters of the Gulf of Mexico," *Environmental Research Letters*, Vol. 6, August 2011.

The effects from the oil spill were spread throughout the Gulf Coast ecosystem. In the immediate aftermath of the spill, more than 88,522 square miles of coastline were closed and almost 1,100 miles of shoreline and related habitat were damaged due to oiling.[13] A map of some of the more notable documented oiling impacts in the immediate area of the oil spill is shown below in **Figure 1**.[14]

Figure 1. Selected Impacts of the Gulf Coast Oil Spill

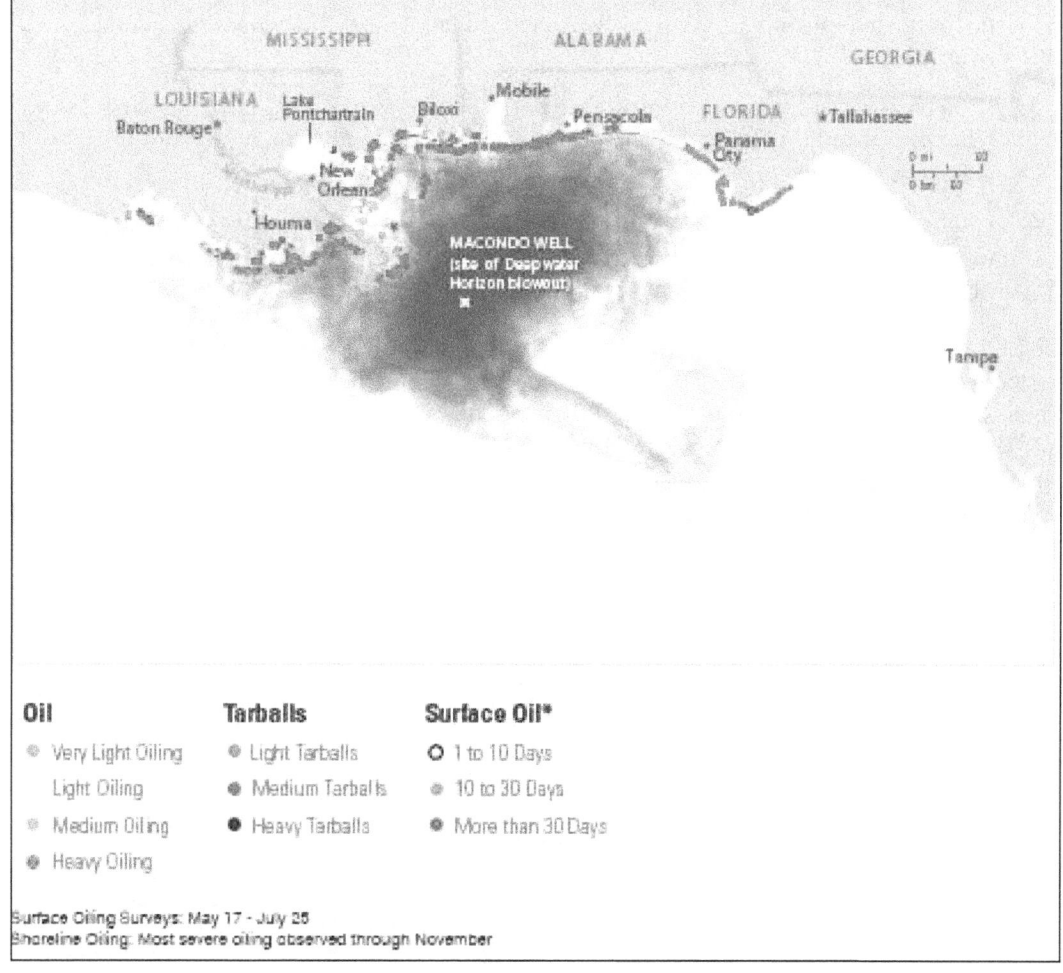

Source: National Commission on the BP Deepwater Horizon Oil Spill and Offshore Drilling, *Deep Water: The Gulf Oil Disaster and the Future of Offshore Drilling*, Report to the President, January 2011.

Several scientists have noted that the long-term effects of the spill are likely to persist into the future.[15] One of the earliest reports on the oil spill, carried out by a presidential task force under

---

[13] Data from CRS communication with National Oceanic and Atmospheric Administration Office of Response and Restoration officials, October 3, 2011 and Mabus Report.

[14] A web-based Geographic Information System tool with relevant monitoring and other data layers is available at http://gomex.erma.noaa.gov/erma html#x=-88.25810&y=27.03211&z=6&layers=19130.

[15] Mabus Report, p. 2.

the direction of former Secretary of the Navy Ray Mabus,[16] divided the effects of the oil spill into four areas:

1. Water Column Effects: Due to the location and scale of the oil spill, the spill is expected to have impacts on the food chain in coastal areas.

2. Fisheries Effects: The oil spill led to the temporary closure of approximately 36% of federal Gulf waters, as well as in-state waters, to fishing. Although these waters have subsequently been reopened, studies on fisheries impacts are ongoing, and impacts from oil on fish eggs and larvae may be better understood over time.

3. Effects on Other Species: Animals face both short-term and long-term impacts from the oil spill, including impacts on food availability, growth, reproduction, behavior, and disease.

4. Habitat Effects: Beaches, wetlands, and other Gulf Coats habitats were exposed to oil, which could potentially exacerbate erosion issues in the region and kill plants and animals.

Specific long-term effects on the ecosystem are still being studied. Documented effects have been reported by scientists for various aspects of the ecosystem. For example, scientists provided estimates on the effect of the oil plume on deep sea sediment habitat and species around the well head. They reported that the most severe reduction of biodiversity in this habitat extended 3 km around the wellhead, and that moderate impacts were observed up to 17 km southwest and 8.5 km northeast of the wellhead.[17] Further, scientists estimated that recovery rates for this habitat could be in terms of decades or longer.[18] The effects on the seafood industry are also being calculated economically and environmentally for the long term. Apart from the shutdown of fisheries due to the immediate effects of the spill, some observers are noting that the seafood catch is less than in previous years and that effects of the spill on younger generations of fisheries populations could result in lower catches in the future when remaining fish mature.

Federal Restoration in the Gulf since the *Deepwater Horizon* Oil Spill

After the oil spill, efforts were focused on addressing the immediate impacts of the oil spill and monitoring how the spill was spreading through the ecosystems. Although the Oil Pollution Act (OPA) liability provisions[19] are meant to address natural resource damages related to the oil spill,

---

[16] See the "Mabus Report" generally. The report is further discussed further in the below section, "Federal Restoration in the Gulf since the Deepwater Horizon Oil Spill."

[17] Paul A. Montagna et al., "Deep-Sea Benthic Footprint of the Deepwater Horizon Blowout," *PLoS ONE*, vol. 8, no. 8 (2013), p. 1.

[18] Ibid.

[19] 33 U.S.C. §2702. This process is discussed in the below section, "

Natural Resource Damages under the Oil Pollution Act"

many policy makers and stakeholders expressed an interest in also addressing pre-spill natural resource issues in the Gulf.[20]

Mabus Report and Gulf Coast Ecosystem Restoration Task Force

The impetus for long-term environmental restoration and recovery efforts related to the oil spill can be traced, in part, to a September 2010 report commissioned by the Obama Administration and under the direction of former Secretary of the Navy Ray Mabus (also known as the "Mabus Report").[21] The report outlined existing processes as well as potential new funding sources for Gulf Coast restoration. The final report noted the multiple challenges facing the Gulf Coast and suggested incorporating them into the response to the oil spill:

> This is a region that was already struggling with urgent environmental challenges.... [I]t only makes sense to look at the broader challenges facing the system and to leverage ongoing efforts to find solutions to some of the complex problems that face the Gulf. Sustained activities that restore the critical ecosystem functions of the Gulf will be needed to support and sustain the region's economic revitalization.[22]

The report made a number of recommendations for future restoration actions to address this challenge. Most importantly, the Mabus Report recommended the dedication of civil penalties under the Clean Water Act toward Gulf restoration to address recovery needs that may fall outside the scope of natural resource damages under the OPA.[23] It further recommended that "Congress establish a Gulf Coast Recovery Council that should focus on improving the economy and public health of the Gulf Coast, and on ecosystem restoration not dealt with under [OPA's Natural Resource Damage Assessment program]. These three areas are inextricably linked to the successful recovery of the region."[24]

To further the long-term restoration objectives outlined in the Mabus Report, the President established the Gulf Coast Ecosystem Restoration Task Force in October 2010.[25] The task force held meetings, met with public officials, and produced a restoration strategy in December 2011, which was expected to guide future restoration efforts in the region.[26] The task force strategy defined ecosystem restoration goals and described milestones towards reaching those goals; considered existing research and ecosystem restoration planning efforts; identified major policy areas where coordinated actions between government agencies were needed; and evaluated existing research and monitoring programs and gaps in data collection. The task force goals for Gulf Coast restoration were:

- restore and conserve habitat;

---

[20] To some degree, Gulf restoration activities may be divided into short-term efforts that address natural resource impacts related to the 2010 oil spill, and long-term recovery efforts that address restoration issues in place well before the 2010 spill. However, in some cases it may be difficult to distinguish pre-spill from post-spill ecosystem issues in the Gulf.

[21] See footnote 6.

[22] Mabus Report, p. 23.

[23] Mabus Report, p. 5.

[24] Mabus Report, p. 5.

[25] Executive Order 13554 in 75 *Federal Register* 62313 (October 8, 2010).

[26] See http://epa.gov/gulfcoasttaskforce/pdfs/GulfCoastReport_Full_12-04_508-1.pdf.

- restore water quality;

- replenish and protect living coastal and marine resources; and

- enhance community resilience.

Enactment of the RESTORE Act in P.L. 112-141 (discussed below) in July 2012 resulted in the creation of the Gulf Coast Ecosystem Restoration Council, and led to the President disbanding the task force.[27]

Environmental and Economic Restoration Efforts and Funding

Since the oil spill, congressional legislation, civil and criminal settlements relating to oil spill damages, and existing federal programs have initiated a number of actions intended to restore the ecosystems and economies in the Gulf Coast region. Many of these actions are related, but have different planning processes and timelines, leadership, and goals. The below sections focus on three significant efforts aimed at environmentally and economically restoring the Gulf Coast region:

- RESTORE Act funding/Gulf Coast Ecosystem Restoration Trust Fund;

- National Fish and Wildlife Foundation (NFWF) Gulf Coast Restoration Funding; and

- Natural Resource Damages under the Oil Pollution Act.

In addition to these efforts, funding for Gulf Restoration activities is also being made available under a number of smaller settlements and through ongoing federal agency activities (as discussed above). A summary of civil and criminal settlements to date and their required funding allocations is provided in the **Appendix** to this report. While economic claims and other payments to individuals damaged by the spill may in some cases be used contribute to or complement the activities discussed below, they are not included in this discussion.[28]

RESTORE Act/Gulf Coast Ecosystem Restoration Trust Fund

The RESTORE Act is a subtitle[29] in legislation (MAP-21) enacted on July 6, 2012 (P.L. 112-141).[30] The RESTORE Act establishes the Gulf Coast Restoration Trust Fund in the General Treasury. Eighty percent of any administrative and civil Clean Water Act (CWA) Section 311[31] penalties paid by responsible parties in connection with the 2010 *Deepwater Horizon* oil spill are

---

[27] See Executive Order 13626 in 77 *Federal Register* 56749 (September 13, 2012). The council, discussed in the below section "30%—Gulf Coast Ecosystem Restoration Council," is composed of the Governors of the five affected Gulf States and the Secretaries of the departments of Interior, Commerce, Agriculture, and Homeland Security, the Secretary of the Army and the Administrator of the Environmental Protection Agency.

[28] For a complete discussion of these claims, see CRS Report R42942, *Deepwater Horizon Oil Spill: Recent Activities and Ongoing Developments*, by Jonathan L. Ramseur and Curry L. Hagerty.

[29] Division A, Title I, Subtitle F.

[30] As discussed below, the effective date of the RESTORE Act provisions, unless otherwise provided, is October 1, 2012.

[31] 33 U.S.C. §1321.

deposited in the fund.[32] Amounts in the Trust Fund will be available for expenditure without further appropriation. The act directs the Secretary of the Treasury to promulgate implementing regulations concerning Trust Fund deposits and expenditures. These regulations were published in draft form on September 6, 2013.[33]

Fund Administration

The RESTORE Act gives the Secretary of the Treasury the authority to determine how much money from the Trust Fund should be expended each fiscal year, and regulations from the Treasury Department have since confirmed this approach. In accordance with the RESTORE Act and Treasury regulations, for each fiscal year the Secretary of the Treasury is to release funds from the Trust Fund toward the required components (discussed below), and invest the remainder "that are not, in the judgment of the Secretary, required to meet needs for current withdrawals."[34] These investments are to be in interest-bearing obligations of the United States with maturities suitable to the needs of the Trust Fund. The Secretary also has the authority to audit and stop expending funds to particular entities (e.g., states), if the Secretary determines funds are not being used for prescribed activities. The authority of the Trust Fund terminates when all funds owed to the Trust Fund have been returned, and all funds from the Trust Fund have been expended.

Funding Distribution and Authorized Uses

The act distributes monies from the Gulf Coast Restoration Fund to various entities through multiple processes, or "components." All of the funds—not counting authorized administrative activities—would support activities in one or more of the five Gulf of Mexico states. The different fund allotments and their conditions are discussed below and illustrated in **Figure 2**. The largest component is the "Direct Component," under which 35% of Trust Fund monies will be distributed directly by Treasury equally to the five states. Other major components include the Council-Selected Restoration Component (also referred to as the "Comprehensive Plan Component"), under which the Council is to receive 30% for an ecosystem restoration plan, and the "Spill Impact" Component, under which the Council will receive an additional 30% but distribute this amount to states unequally. Two other smaller allocations go toward science and research grants (2.5%, respectively). Each of these components is discussed in detail below. Pursuant to the Treasury regulations, no more than 3% of the amount received by the Council and other political subdivisions (e.g., states, counties) for any of these components may be used for administrative expenses.

---

[32] If not for the RESTORE Act, revenues from these penalties would support the Oil Spill Liability Trust Fund (OSLTF)—pursuant to 26 U.S.C. §9509.

[33] Department of the Treasury, 78 *Federal Register* 5801, September 6, 2013. http://federalregister.gov/a/2013-21595. Hereinafter "78 *Federal Register* 5801."

[34] 78 *Federal Register* 5801.

Figure 2. RESTORE Act Distribution of Clean Water Act Penalties

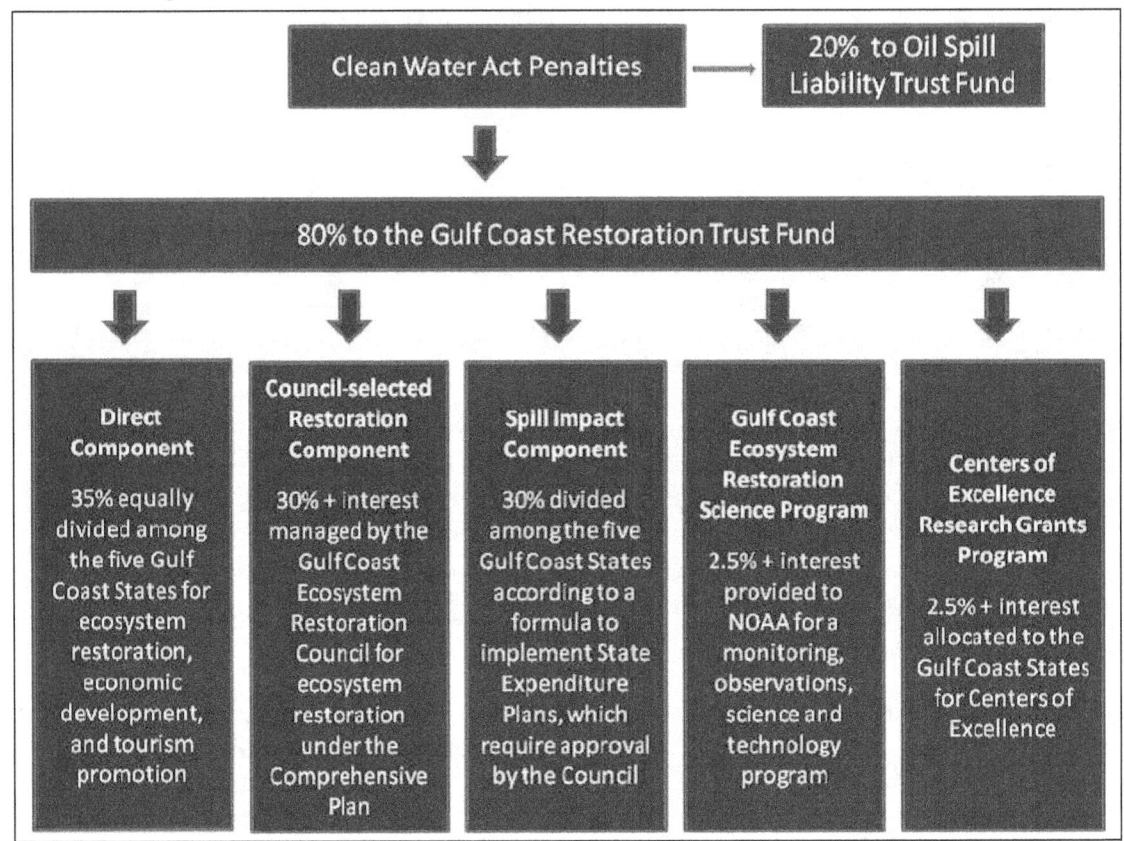

Source: Gulf Coast Restoration Council, Initial Comprehensive Plan.

35%—Direct Component: Equal Shares to the Five Gulf States

The largest portion of the fund (35%, other than interest earned on investments) is to be divided equally among the five Gulf of Mexico states: Alabama, Florida, Louisiana, Mississippi, and Texas. The Treasury will provide this funding as grants to these states in a given fiscal year. The act has further requirements for specific distributions to political subdivisions in Florida and Louisiana. In Florida, the shares are to be divided among affected counties, with 75% of that state's share to be distributed to the eight "disproportionately affected" counties while the remaining 25% will go to "non-disproportionately impacted" counties. In Louisiana, 30% of its share goes to individual parishes based on a statutory formula, and the remainder goes to the state Coastal Protection and Restoration Authority Board. For other states, all of the funding will be distributed to similar state authorities or offices.[35]

The act stipulates that the state (or county) funding must be applied toward one or more of the following 11 activities:[36]

---

[35] This includes: for Alabama, the Alabama Gulf Coast Recovery Council; for Mississippi, the Mississippi Department of Environmental Quality; and for Texas, the Office of the Governor.

[36] 33 U.S.C. §1321(t)(1)(B)

- Restoration and protection of the natural resources, ecosystems, fisheries, marine and wildlife habitats, beaches, and coastal wetlands of the Gulf Coast region.

- Mitigation of damage to fish, wildlife, and natural resources.

- Implementation of a federally approved marine, coastal, or comprehensive conservation management plan, including fisheries monitoring.

- Workforce development and job creation.

- Improvements to or on state parks located in coastal areas affected by the *Deepwater Horizon* oil spill.

- Infrastructure projects benefitting the economy or ecological resources, including port infrastructure.

- Coastal flood protection and related infrastructure.

- Planning assistance.

- Administrative costs (limited to not more than 3% of a state's allotment).

- Promotion of tourism in the Gulf Coast Region, including recreational fishing.

- Promotion of the consumption of seafood harvested from the Gulf Coast Region.

Subsequently, the Treasury regulations for the program outlined a similar set of activities, but noted that the first six activities above are only eligible to the extent they are carried out in the Gulf Coast Region.[37] To receive its share of funds (which are to be distributed as a grant), a state must meet several conditions, including a certification (as determined by the Secretary of the Treasury) that, among other things, funds are applied to one of the above activities and that activities are selected through public input. In addition, states must submit a multi-year implementation plan, documenting activities for which they receive funding.

The RESTORE Act further stipulates that each state must agree to meet conditions for receiving funds that are promulgated by the Secretary of the Treasury, and certify that requested projects meet certain conditions.[38] These conditions include that projects (1) are designed to restore and protect natural resources of the Gulf Coast environment or economy; (2) carry out one or more of the 11 activities described above; (3) were selected with public input; and (4) are based on the best available science. Under the RESTORE Act, the states are required to develop and submit a multi-year implementation plan for the use of received funds, which may include milestones, projected completion of the project, and mechanisms to evaluate progress.[39] States can also use funds to satisfy requirements for the non-federal cost share of authorized federal projects.[40]

---

[37] The Treasury Regulations define "Gulf Coast Region" as coastal zones defined under Section 304 of the Coastal Zone Management Act of 1972 that border the Gulf of Mexico; land within the coastal zones held in trust by the Federal Government; adjacent land, water, and watersheds within 25 miles of the coastal zone, and all federal waters in the Gulf of Mexico.

[38] 33 U.S.C. §1321(t)(1)(E).

[39] 33 U.S.C. §1321(t)(1)(E)(iv).

[40] 33 U.S.C. §1321(t)(1)(J).

30%—*Gulf Coast Ecosystem Restoration Council Comprehensive Plan*

The RESTORE Act authorizes the creation of a new council to govern the majority of ecosystem restoration efforts under the bill. The council is named the Gulf Coast Ecosystem Restoration Council and contains representatives from high-level officials from six federal agencies and the governor (or his/her designee) from each of the five Gulf Coast states. The act provides for the distribution of 30% of all revenues of the Trust Fund, plus one-half of the interest earned on investments, to the Council to fund a comprehensive ecosystem restoration plan (termed the Comprehensive Plan). In addition to allocating this funding towards restoration, the Council is also responsible for allocating 30% of the Trust Fund to Gulf States under a formula established in the RESTORE Act (see next section for details). The Council is authorized to conduct several actions, including developing and revising the Comprehensive Plan; identifying conceived projects prior to enactment that could restore the ecosystem quickly; establishing advisory committees; collecting and considering scientific research, and submitting reports to Congress.

After a series of public meetings, on May 23, 2013, the Council released a Draft Initial Comprehensive Plan.[41] The plan set in motion a series of subsequent public meetings and a formal comment period. The plan was finalized by the Council on August 28, 2013.[42] The Comprehensive Plan establishes five broad restoration goals and details how the Council will select and fund projects. Project selection criteria and evaluation reflects provisions under the RESTORE Act. The Plan is to address restoration under two components: the Restoration Component and the Spill Impact Component. Each component reflects conditions and criteria established under the RESTORE Act for funding. The Plan notes that selected projects under the Restoration Component might not be balanced according to the restoration goals.[43] For example, projects that aim to restore, improve, and protect water quality (one of the goals) might out-number projects that aim to restore and enhance natural processes and shorelines (another goal). Further, according to the Plan and the RESTORE Act, the responsibility for implementing a project under the Plan is to be given to either a state or a federal agency. Therefore, the Council may not be considered an implementing entity, but rather a managing and oversight entity for restoration. This is similar to other restoration initiatives such as in the Great Lakes, where funds are disseminated to agencies or other stakeholders based on proposed projects and activities.

The Initial Comprehensive Plan does not include a description of how funds from the Trust Fund will be allocated to implement the plan over the next 10 years. This element is referred to in the plan as the "Ten-Year Funding Strategy," and was required under the RESTORE Act.[44] Further, the Plan does not contain a project and program priority list that the Council would be expected to fund over the next three years as required under the RESTORE Act. This is referred to as the "Funded Priorities List," and was also required under the RESTORE Act.[45] The Plan states that these provisions were not met due to uncertainty over how much funds will be deposited into the Trust Fund, the absence of procedures for how funds will be distributed to the Council (this is

---

[41] A draft version of the Initial Comprehensive Plan is available at http://www.restorethegulf.gov/sites/default/files/ Gulf%20Restoration%20Council%20Draft%20Initial%20Comprehensive%20Plan%205.23.15.pdf. This version of the Plan was the version that was finalized on August 28. Hereinafter, *Initial Comprehensive Plan*.

[42] Minutes of the August 28 meeting, including outside comments, are available at http://www.restorethegulf.gov/ release/2013/08/21/gulf-coast-ecosystem-restoration-council-posts-materials-august-28-2013-council-m.

[43] *Initial Comprehensive Plan*, p. 9.

[44] 33 U.S.C. §1321(t)(2)(D)(ii)(IV)(cc).

[45] 33 U.S.C. §1321(t)(2)(D)(ii)(IV)(dd).

referred to as the Treasury regulations and a proposed version was released after the Draft Plan was released), lack of public input into these two public documents, and lack of State Expenditure Plans.[46] Regulations by the Department of the Treasury have clarified eligible activities for the Comprehensive Plan to include activities in the Gulf Coast Region that would restore and protect the natural resources, ecosystems, fisheries, marine and wildlife habitats, beaches, coastal wetlands, and economy of the Gulf Coast Region.

30%—Spill Impact Component: Unequal Shares to the Five Gulf States

The act directs the Council to disburse 30% of Trust Fund monies to the five Gulf States based on the relative impact of the oil spill in each state. The Council is to develop a distribution formula based on criteria listed in the act. In general, the criteria involve a measure of shoreline impact; oiled shoreline distance from the *Deepwater Horizon* rig; and coastal population.[47] To date, there have been no authoritative estimates of the amount to be provided to each state under these criteria.

To receive funding, each state must submit a plan for approval to the Council. State plans must document how funding will support one or more of the 11 categories listed in the Direct Component section above. Information and criteria for developing the state plans are included in the Initial Comprehensive Plan. However, in contrast to the Direct Component, only 25% of a state's funding can be used to support infrastructure projects in categories six (infrastructure projects benefitting the economy or ecological resources, including port infrastructure) and seven (coastal flood protection and related infrastructure).[48]

2.5%—Gulf Coast Ecosystem Restoration Science, Observation, Monitoring, and Technology (GCERSOMT) Program

The act establishes the Gulf Coast Ecosystem Restoration Science, Observation, Monitoring, and Technology (GCERSOMT) program, funded by 2.5% of monies in the Trust Fund. The National Oceanic and Atmospheric Administration (NOAA) Administrator will implement the program, which is to support marine research projects that pertain to species in the Gulf of Mexico. Further, the Program is to conduct monitoring and research on marine and estuarine ecosystems; and collect data and stock assessments on fisheries and other marine and estuarine variables. There is an emphasis on coordination with other entities to conduct this work and provisions that instruct the Administrator to avoid duplication of efforts. This program is to sunset when all funds in the Trust Fund are expended.

2.5%—Centers of Excellence

The act disburses 2.5% of monies in the Trust Fund to the five Gulf States to establish—through a competitive grant program—Centers of Excellence. The centers would be nongovernmental entities (including public or private institutions) and consortia in the Gulf Coast Region. Centers

---

[46] *Initial Comprehensive Plan*, p. 2.

[47] See 33 U.S.C. §1321(t)(3)(A)(ii).

[48] The act allows states to spend more than 25% of their funding on infrastructure if the state certifies the projects will meet particular conditions.

of Excellence are to focus on science, technology, and monitoring in at least one of the following areas: Coastal and deltaic sustainability and restoration and protection; coastal fisheries and wildlife ecosystem research and monitoring in the Gulf Coast region; sustainable and economic growth and commercial development in the region; and mapping and monitoring of the Gulf of Mexico water body.

Interest Earned by the Fund

Interest earned by the Trust Fund would be distributed as follows:

- 50% would fund the Gulf Coast Ecosystem Restoration Council to implement the Comprehensive Plan.

- 25% would provide additional funding for the Gulf Coast Ecosystem Restoration Science, Observation, Monitoring, and Technology program mentioned above.

- 25% would provide additional funding for the Centers of Excellence research grants mentioned above.

Funding Levels

The total amount of revenue that would be available to finance the Gulf Coast Restoration Trust Fund is uncertain (see box below). As of the date of this report, only Transocean has announced a civil settlement with the federal government.[49] As a result of the settlement of the Transocean claims, a total of $800 million, plus interest, is expected to be deposited into the Trust Fund within the next two years. However BP's civil penalties under the Clean Water Act, which could be considerable, are yet to be determined.

---

[49] A table of settlements as of the date of this report is provided in the Appendix.

Uncertain Funding Levels Resulting from the BP Civil Settlement

CWA Section 311 authorizes certain civil judicial penalties for the owner, operator, or person in charge of a vessel, onshore facility, or offshore facility for violations of that provision. A civil judicial penalty applies to a violation of the CWA prohibition on discharging oil into navigable waters of the United States. The monetary penalty for this violation may be up to $37,500 per day of violation, or up to $1,100 per barrel discharged. If the violation is deemed a result of gross negligence or willful misconduct, the penalty is not less than $140,000 for the violation, nor more than $4,300 per barrel discharged.

According to the most recent estimate from the federal government, the 2010 oil spill resulted in a discharge of approximately 206 million gallons (4.9 million barrels) in the Gulf of Mexico.[50] However, BP argued that an estimated 17% of the 4.9 million barrels did not enter the Gulf environment, but was directly recovered from the wellhead by BP. In February 2013, the federal government agreed with BP that this volume of oil would not be considered toward the CWA penalty determination.[51]

The $1,100 to $4,300 per-barrel range is the basis of the oft-cited judicial penalty range for the 2010 *Deepwater Horizon* oil spill: $4.5 billion to $21.5 billion.[52] However, based on the February 2013 agreement (above) the upper end of the range would be approximately $17.6 billion. The low end of this range is achieved by multiplying 4.1 million barrels (amount of discharge after removing the 17% directly captured by BP) by $1,100/ barrel. The upper end of the range is achieved by multiplying 4.1 million barrels (total discharge amount minus amount directly recovered) by the maximum penalty of $4,300/barrel, which presumes a determination of either gross negligence or willful misconduct.

In addition, when determining the amount of the judicial penalty, CWA Section 311(b)(8)[53] states that "the Environmental Protection Agency (EPA) Administrator, the Secretary [of Homeland Security],[54] or the court, as the case may be," must consider the following factors:

- the seriousness of the violation or violations;
- the economic benefit to the violator, if any, resulting from the violation;
- the degree of culpability involved;
- any other penalty for the same incident;
- any history of prior violations;
- the nature, extent, and degree of success of any efforts of the violator to minimize or mitigate the effects of the discharge;
- the economic impact of the penalty on the violator; and
- any other matters as justice may require.

Therefore, the judicial civil penalty for the incident could be less than the low end of the above range ($4.5 billion), even if gross negligence or willful misconduct is determined.

---

[50] Federal Interagency Solutions Group, Oil Budget Calculator Science and Engineering Team. *Oil Budget Calculator: Deepwater Horizon-Technical Documentation*. November 2010. See also CRS Report R41531, *Deepwater Horizon Oil Spill: The Fate of the Oil*, by Jonathan L. Ramseur.

[51] United States District Court, Eastern District of Louisiana, Stipulation Mooting BP's Motion for Partial Summary Judgement, February 19, 2013, at http://www.laed.uscourts.gov/OilSpill/OilSpill.htm.

[52] National Commission on the BP Deepwater Horizon Oil Spill and Offshore Drilling, *Deep Water: The Gulf Oil Disaster and the Future of Offshore Drilling*. Report to the President, January 2011, p. 211.

[53] 33 U.S.C. §1321(b)(8).

[54] The Coast Guard is part of the Department of Homeland Security.

Status

As noted above, the Gulf Coast Ecosystem Restoration Council voted unanimously to adopt the draft version of the Initial Comprehensive Plan on August 28, 2013. The plan established overarching goals based on the aforementioned Mabus Report[55] and broad evaluation and selection criteria on which it plans to base its decisions. In accordance with the RESTORE Act, the plan included a preliminary list of authorized but not yet commenced projects and programs which may be eligible for funding (including projects at the local, state, and federal levels), but did not include any project selections under the Funded Priorities List or the Ten-Year Funding Strategy due to funding uncertainty.[56] The Council is expected to further develop the Initial Comprehensive Plan as existing uncertainties are resolved (e.g., how much money is to be deposited into the Trust Fund). Further, the Council states that it will be working on establishing an Oil Spill Restoration Impact Allocation formula, Ten-Year Funding Strategy, Funded Priorities List, and advisory committees as needed.[57]

National Fish and Wildlife Foundation Funding

The National Fish and Wildlife Foundation (NFWF) was established by Congress in 1984. It is an independent 501(c)(3) nonprofit organization governed by a 30-member Board of Directors.[58] The NFWF board is approved by the Secretary of the Interior and includes the Director of the Fish and Wildlife Service. NFWF typically receives limited federal funds which it uses to leverage grants for conservation purposes. NFWF also administers mitigation funds targeted to specific sites or projects, including roughly 160 different funds as of June 2013.[59]

Pursuant to the criminal settlements between BP and DOJ and between Transocean and DOJ in early 2013, NFWF is scheduled to receive over $2.5 billion for Gulf Coast restoration over the five-year period from 2013 to 2017.[60] Both criminal plea documents direct NFWF to use the funds in the following manner:

- 50% (approximately $1.3 billion) of the funds is to support the creation or restoration of barrier islands off the coast of Louisiana and implementation of river diversion projects to create, preserve, or restore coastal habitats. These projects will "remedy harm to resources where there has been injury to, or destruction of, loss of, or loss of use of those resources resulting from the [*Deepwater Horizon*] oil spill."

---

[55] The five goals established by the plan were: restore and conserve habitat; restore water quality; replenish and protect living coastal and marine resources; enhance community resilience, and restore and revitalize the Gulf economy.

[56] As discussed previously, these elements were required under the RESTORE Act, Section 1603 (2)(D)(ii)(IV); under the act, the three-year Funded Priorities list was required "subject to available funding." The list of authorized but not yet commenced projects is available at http://www restorethegulf.gov/sites/default/files/
Appendix%20A_Background%20Information%20-
%20Preliminary%20List%20of%20Authorized%20but%20Not%20Commenced%20Projects%20and%20Programs.pdf

[57] *Comprehensive Plan*, p. 20.

[58] For more information about this organization, see http://www nfwf.org.

[59] Statement of Jeff Trandahl, Executive Director, National Fish and Wildlife Foundation. U.S. Congress, Senate Committee on Commerce, Science, and Transportation, *Gulf Restoration: A Progress Report 3 Years After the Deepwater Horizon Disaster*, 113th Cong., 1st sess., June 6, 2013. Hereinafter, *Trandahl Statement, 2013*.

[60] The Transocean monies are scheduled to be disbursed over a two-year period, and the BP monies are scheduled to come in over a five-year period.

- 50% of the funds are to support projects that "remedy harm to resources where there has been injury to, or destruction of, loss of, or loss of use of those resources resulting from the [*Deepwater Horizon*] oil spill." NFWF will support such projects in the Gulf states based on the following proportions: Alabama, 28% ($356 million); Florida, 28% ($356 million); Mississippi, 28% ($356 million); and Texas, 16% ($203 million).

Of these funds, the vast majority are expected to be made available to NFWF in the fourth and fifth years (2017 and 2018). The payment schedule and allocations to individual states are shown below in **Table 1**. For both the BP and Transocean settlement allocations, NFWF is directed to consult with "appropriate state resource managers, as well as federal resource managers that have the statutory authority for coordination or cooperation with private entities, to identify projects and to maximize the environmental benefits of such projects." For the Louisiana projects, NFWF is directed to consider the State Coastal Master Plan, as well as the Louisiana Coastal Area Mississippi River Hydrodynamic and Delta Management Study, as appropriate.[61]

Table 1. Schedule of Payments to NFWF Gulf Environmental Benefit Fund

(payments from BP and Transocean settlements in millions of dollars)

Date	Louisiana	Alabama	Florida	Mississippi	Texas	Total Payment
Apr 2013	$79.00	$22.12	$22.12	$22.12	$12.64	**$158.00**
Feb 2014	176.50	49.42	49.42	49.42	28.24	**353.00**
Feb 2015	169.50	47.46	47.46	47.46	27.12	**339.00**
Feb 2016	150.00	42.00	42.00	42.00	24.00	**300.00**
Feb 2017	250.00	70.00	70.00	70.00	40.00	**500.00**
Feb 2018	474.00	125.16	125.16	125.16	71.52	**894.00**
Totals	**$1,272.00**	**$356.16**	**$356.16**	**$356.16**	**$203.52**	**$2,544.00**

Source: National Fish and Wildlife Foundation.

Status

NFWF established the Gulf Environmental Benefit Fund (Gulf Fund) to receive funding to carry out Gulf Coast restoration efforts under the settlement. NFWF also reported that it is consulting with state and federal natural resource management agencies involved in other Gulf Coast restoration efforts (e.g., RESTORE and Natural Resource Damage processes). The first projects under the Gulf fund were announced in November 2013. The 22 projects listed are to be in the states of Alabama, Florida, Louisiana, Mississippi, and Texas, and were expected to cost an estimated $100 million in total.[62]

---

[61] More information is available from NFWF at http://www.nfwf.org/Pages/gulf/Gulf-Environmental-Benefit-Fund.aspx.

[62] NFWF Press Release: NFWF Announces More Than $100 Million for Resteoration Projects on the Gulf Coast. November 14, 2013. http://www.nfwf.org/whoweare/mediacenter/pr/Pages/NFWF-Announces-More-Than-$100-Million-.aspx.

Natural Resource Damages under the Oil Pollution Act[63]

The Oil Pollution Act (OPA), which became law after the *Exxon Valdez* oil spill of 1989, allows state, federal, and tribal governments to act as "trustees" to recover damages to natural resources in the public trust from the parties responsible for an oil spill. Under the OPA, responsible parties are liable for damages to natural resources, the measure of which includes:

- the cost of restoring, rehabilitating, replacing, or acquiring the equivalent of the damaged natural resources;

- the diminution in value of those natural resources pending restoration;

- the reasonable cost of assessing those damages.[64]

The National Oceanic and Atmospheric Administration (NOAA) developed regulations pertaining to the process for natural resource damage assessment (NRDA) under the OPA in 1996.[65] Natural resource damages may include both losses of direct use and passive uses. Direct use value may derive from recreational (e.g., boating), commercial (e.g., fishing), or cultural or historical uses of the resource. In contrast, a passive-use value may derive from preserving the resource for its own sake or for enjoyment by future generations.[66]

The damages are compensatory, not punitive. Collected damages cannot be placed into the general Treasury revenues of the federal or state government, but must be used to restore or replace lost resources.[67] Indeed, NOAA's regulations focus on the costs of primary restoration—returning the resource to its baseline condition—and compensatory restoration—addressing interim losses of resources and their services.[68]

The *Deepwater Horizon* NRDA Trustees are:

- the United States Department of the Interior (DOI);

- the National Oceanic and Atmospheric Administration (NOAA), on behalf of the United States Department of Commerce;

- the State of Louisiana's Coastal Protection and Restoration Authority, Oil Spill Coordinator's Office, Department of Environmental Quality, Department of Wildlife and Fisheries, and Department of Natural Resources;

- the State of Mississippi's Department of Environmental Quality;

- the State of Alabama's Department of Conservation and Natural Resources and Geological Survey of Alabama;

---

[63] For more information on the NRDA process as it relates to the *Deepwater Horizon* spill, see CRS Report R41972, *The 2010 Deepwater Horizon Oil Spill: Natural Resource Damage Assessment Under the Oil Pollution Act*, by Adam Vann and Robert Meltz

[64] 33 U.S.C. §2706(d).

[65] 61 *Federal Register* 440 (January 5, 1996). See also NOAA, *Injury Assessment Guidance Document for Natural Resource Damage Assessment Under the Oil Pollution Act of 1990* (1996).

[66] See 15 C.F.R. §990.30, definition of "value."

[67] 33 U.S.C. §2706(f).

[68] See William D. Brighton, *Natural Resource Damages under the Comprehensive Environmental Response, Compensation, and Liability Act*, U.S. Department of Justice, Environment and Natural Resources Division, 2006.

- the State of Florida's Department of Environmental Protection and Fish and Wildlife Conservation Commission; and

- for the State of Texas: Texas Parks and Wildlife Department, Texas General Land Office, and Texas Commission on Environmental Quality.

NRDA Process

When a spill occurs, natural resource trustees conduct a natural resource damage assessment to determine the extent of the harm. Trustees may include officials from federal agencies designated by the President, state agencies designated by the relevant governor, and representatives from tribal and foreign governments.

The trustees' work occurs in three steps: a Pre-assessment Phase, the Restoration Planning Phase, and the Restoration Implementation Phase. The *Deepwater Horizon* NRDA process is in the restoration planning phase. During this phase, the trustees quantify injuries and identify possible restoration projects.[69] This process can take years, especially for complex incidents like the 2010 Gulf oil spill. However, during the NRDA process, early restoration projects can be completed to begin restoration of natural resources sooner than might otherwise be possible. This has been the case during the *Deepwater Horizon* NRDA process.

Status

The NRDA evaluation process is ongoing; however, as noted above, early restoration projects may be initiated in the meantime to allow for expedited restoration activities. On April 21, 2011, the trustees for the *Deepwater Horizon* oil spill announced an agreement with BP to provide $1 billion toward early restoration projects in the Gulf of Mexico to address injuries to natural resources caused by the spill. The agreement, known as the "Framework for Early Restoration Addressing Injuries Resulting from the Deepwater Horizon Oil Spill" (or the Framework Agreement), provided the basis for subsequent early restoration actions.[70] Under the Framework Agreement, a proposed Early Restoration project may be funded only if all of the Trustees, the U.S. Department of Justice, and BP agree on, among other things, the amount of funding to be provided by BP and the Natural Resources Damages (NRD) Offsets (or NRD Offsets) that will be credited for that project against BP's liability for damages resulting from the spill. Following announcement of the Framework Agreement in 2011, the NRDA trustees solicited projects from the public through meetings and the Internet. A summary of projects funded to date is provided below.

Dissemination of early restoration funds has been divided into three phases. As of January 2014, the first two phases of early restoration were complete, resulting in funding 10 projects with a total estimated cost of approximately $71 million.[71] On May 6, 2013, the trustees issued a notice

---

[69] For more updated information, see NOAA's website at http://www.gulfspillrestoration noaa.gov/oil-spill/.

[70] Department of the Interior et al., *Deepwater Horizon Oil Spill Draft Programmatic and Phase III Early Restoration Plan and Draft Restoration Programmatic Environmental Impact Statement*, Washington, DC, December 2013, http://www.gulfspillrestoration noaa.gov/restoration/early-restoration/phase-iii/.

[71] See Phase I (April 2012) and Phase II (October 2012) Early Restoration Plans, at http://www.gulfspillrestoration noaa.gov/.

---

in the *Federal Register* that included additional proposed projects under a proposed Phase III.[72] The draft plan for these projects, released in December 2013, proposes funding an additional 44 early restoration projects at a cost of approximately $627 million. Thus, as of January 2014, the total funding allocated or spent on early restoration projects was $698 million for 54 projects.[73]

Other Settlement Funding for Gulf Coast Restoration

In addition to the major restoration processes and funding mechanisms, civil and criminal pleas have also provided funding to other programs. This funding is generally of lesser magnitude than the RESTORE Act funding, the NFWF funding, and the NRDA funding, but is expected to inform and complement this funding. To date, these funding allocations include:

- $500 million to the National Academy of Sciences from the Transocean and BP criminal plea agreements, to be used for research on human health and environmental protection in the Gulf Region. It is also to be used for research on oil spill prevention and spill response strategies in the Gulf.

- $100 million to the North American Wetlands Conservation Fund from the BP criminal plea agreement for wetlands restoration, conservation, and projects benefiting migratory birds.

Potential Issues, Questions for Congress

The restoration initiative in the Gulf Coast region is still in its early stages. Many of the ongoing Gulf Coast restoration efforts discussed above have yet to be finalized, and the planning processes and funds available for deposit into the Trust Fund have yet to be fully determined. Further, project priority lists, state implementation plans, and other required restoration planning documents are still being developed. Nevertheless, a number of issues may be of interest to Congress in its oversight role related to Gulf Coast restoration. Some of these issues include the coordination of restoration activities among implementing entities; the development and implementation of a comprehensive plan for restoration; governance of restoration activities; and the balancing of the dual goals of ecological restoration and economic development in the Gulf Coast region.

Coordination

The coordination of restoration efforts among the multiple implementing entities in the Gulf Coast region could be one issue of congressional interest. As discussed above, several disparate streams of funding and resources are going toward new and pre-existing restoration activities in the Gulf. These restoration activities are to be planned and implemented according to multiple

---

[72] 78 *Federal Register* 26319, May 6, 2013.

[73] For Phase III (the largest phase to date), proposed projects are in 12 categories: (1) Create and Improve Wetlands; (2) Protect Shorelines and Reduce Erosion; (3) Restore Barrier Islands and Beaches; (4) Restore and Protect Submerged Aquatic Vegetation; (5) Conserve Habitat; (6) Restore Oysters; (7) Restore and Protect Finfish and Shellfish; (8) Restore and Protect Birds; (9) Restore and Protect Sea Turtles; (10) Enhance Public Access to Natural Resources for Recreational Use; (11) Enhance Recreational Experiences; (12) Promote Environmental and Cultural Stewardship, Education and Outreach.

planning documents and processes. For example, efforts conducted by NFWF will be done under its planning process after consultation with state and federal entities, while the Council will be conducting its own coordination with state and federal agencies and governments for disbursing funds from the Trust Fund pursuant to the RESTORE Act. While the primary entities have highlighted coordination of their efforts, there is no formal entity that oversees all ongoing restoration in the Gulf, nor is there a formal coordination process required among the implementing entities. This lack of formal requirements may cause some concerns among some related to the potential duplication of projects, implementation of restoration projects that address the same issue yet promote different solutions, or projects with conflicting goals at local and regional levels.

The Initial Comprehensive Plan under the RESTORE Act acknowledges some of these potential shortfalls and discusses the intention of the Council to coordinate among implementing entities. For example, in the Comprehensive Plan it states that the Council will strive to coordinate with other partners involved in restoration activities to "advance common goals, avoid duplication, and maximize benefits."[74] The RESTORE Act itself also includes some requirements related to coordination, although it does not provide for a congressionally authorized coordinating entity with authority over all relevant processes going forward.[75] The act authorizes memoranda of understanding between the Council and federal agencies to establish integrated funding and implementation plans, which could reduce project duplication and promote an integrated restoration effort among federal entities.[76] It also addresses duplication of efforts in relation to monitoring the Gulf Coast ecosystem. The RESTORE Act requires the Gulf Coast science program to avoid duplication of other research and monitoring activities and requires the Administrator of NOAA to develop a plan for the coordination of projects and activities between the program and other similar state and federal programs and Centers of Excellence.[77]

Broader questions of coordination among restoration activities go beyond the RESTORE Act and may include, in addition to NRDA and NFWF activities, existing federal and state projects and activities, as well as activities conducted in other states that might have an effect in the Gulf Coast region. Some potential questions addressing coordination could include:

- How will restoration plans and projects be coordinated among implementing entities? Is there a need for a congressionally authorized mechanism for coordination?

- How will new restoration activities authorized under the RESTORE Act integrate with existing restoration programs and efforts, without causing overlap?

- Will there be assurances that project monitoring and oversight are measured with similar metrics? Will data and results from restoration activities be comparable to similar activities implemented by another entity?

- Will baseline ecosystem restoration activities continue under their authorities and funding or will they be integrated into efforts authorized under the RESTORE Act and other *Deepwater Horizon* related restoration activities?

---

[74] *Initial Comprehensive Plan,* p. 10.

[75] The act directed coordination between the Council and the Task Force when developing the Comprehensive Plan, but the Task Force has since been discontinued.

[76] 33 U.S.C. §1321(t)(2)(F).

[77] 33 U.S.C. §1321 note.

Planning

Another potential issue for Congress is the status and content of multiple planning processes related to Gulf Restoration. While the planning process under the RESTORE Act may receive significant attention from Congress, planning under the NFWF and NRDA processes may be of interest to some in Congress, as well.

As discussed previously, the Gulf Coast Ecosystem Restoration Council finalized its Initial Comprehensive Plan for restoration in August 2013. The stated intent of the Plan is to provide a framework to implement restoration activities in the Gulf Coast region. The Plan was not considered "complete" at this time. When it was published, the Council noted: "This Plan is the first version of a Plan that will change over time.... Over the next few years, development and implementation of this Plan will be an iterative process leading to a comprehensive region-wide, multi-objective restoration plan based on the best available science."[78]

As previously noted, the Initial Comprehensive Plan published by the Gulf Coast Ecosystem Restoration Council did not include some of the elements required by Congress. While it included a description of the process underpinning project selection and state expenditure plans and a preliminary list of authorized but not commenced projects, it did not include congressionally required elements such as the 10-year funding strategy and the 3-year funded priorities list. According to the Council, this was due to uncertainty related to the amount of funding available for restoration pursuant to settlement or adjudication of claims against parties responsible for the *Deepwater Horizon* spill. Additionally, other elements that are related to Gulf Coast restoration were not required by Congress to be included in the report. For instance, the Initial Comprehensive Plan was not required to include the Direct Component under the RESTORE Act (i.e., funding which goes directly to states). Similarly, activities under the Science Program and Centers of Excellence are not included in this plan (nor are they required to be).

The two other Gulf Coast restoration planning processes discussed in this report are those coordinated by NFWF and NRDA trustees, respectively. Notably, neither are governed by RESTORE Act planning. NFWF restoration actions are governed first by the criminal settlements between DOJ and BP and DOJ and Transocean (and subsequent guidance from NFWF), while the NRDA planning process is governed by NOAA regulations, pursuant to the Oil Pollution Act. These planning processes may be more targeted than much of that which will be provided under the RESTORE Act, and are expected to proceed independently.

The current approach to ecosystem restoration in the Gulf has differences and similarities compared to that which has been carried out in other areas. For instance, in the Everglades, restoration is federally led and ostensibly guided by a centralized, "comprehensive" plan, known as the Comprehensive Everglades Restoration Plan (CERP). Authorized in the Water Resources Development Act of 2000 (P.L. 106-541), CERP outlined 68 distinct projects that are intended to comprise a large amount of the restoration effort. Generally speaking, CERP is more centralized and detailed than the comprehensive planning process that has been carried out for the Gulf under the RESTORE Act to date. However, it is similar to the current planning process in the Gulf in that it is dependent on other restoration efforts that are not formally covered by CERP or led by the federal government.[79] In the case of the Everglades, planning for these activities is

---

[78] *Comprehensive Plan*, p. 1.

[79] For instance, restoration of the Everglades also depends on "non-CERP" restoration in Everglades National Park, the (continued...)

coordinated by a separate congressionally authorized body, the South Florida Ecosystem Restoration Task Force.[80] Whether the Council or some other entity can or should operate in a similar capacity is one potential issue for Congress.

A complete comparison of the disparate planning processes in the Gulf is made difficult by the absence of some information from the processes. For instance, to date no plans have provided an estimated timeframe for completing restoration, nor have they addressed the maintenance of restoration activities when funding has been exhausted and governance structures have been dissolved. Finally, while the processes under NRDA and NFWF have released initial partial lists of restoration projects, no such planning document is yet available for planning under the RESTORE Act (in part due to the lack of funding pursuant to settlements in this area). Potential questions for Congress related to planning for restoration may include:

- Will the planning process under the RESTORE Act incorporate that under other processes, such as that related to pre-spill restoration activities, or restoration activities conducted by states and other entities such as NFWF or under NRDA?

- Will there be a formal planning process for restoration projects of various types?

- When will annual and 10-year project lists be released, as required under the RESTORE Act?

- Will a vision or set of criteria for defining what a restored ecosystem will look like be created or required under RESTORE Act and other planning processes in the Gulf? Will it include an estimate of how long restoration will take or how much it will cost?

- Who will be responsible for providing future funding to continue restoration activities in the Gulf after activities funded under the *Deepwater Horizon* settlements are complete?

- Outside of the 3% limit on administrative expenditures, will there be limits for other expenditure types?

Implementation

Implementation and governance of restoration activities in the Gulf is another important aspect of restoration that is still under development by various entities involved in the Gulf Coast. Several questions related to implementation of activities could be posed, including questions on the division of labor between federal and state activities, how progress will be measured, and the timing of activities going forward.

As discussed previously, restoration activities in the Gulf Region will be implemented by several federal, state, and non-governmental entities under different structures. The RESTORE Act does not specify an overarching entity that would monitor and report on the implementation of all aspects of restoration. The Council's responsibility appears to be focused on the implementation

---

(...continued)

Central Everglades and water quality projects being carried out by the State of Florida.

[80] The task force was authorized under the Water Resources Development Act of 1996 (P.L. 104-303), Section 528(f) and consists of 14 members from federal state, tribal, and local governments.

of the Comprehensive Plan and state plans pursuant to the Spill Impact Component, while NRDA and NFWF plans will focus on those elements separately.[81] This could raise questions about how restoration activities derived from various funding streams relate to each other. For example:

- Will any entity be responsible for evaluating and reporting on the overall status of restoration activities in the Gulf, or will reporting be conducted separately?

- If restoration crosses state borders, will there be oversight to determine if restoration activities among states are complementary or contrasting?

- How will conflicting implementation objectives be handled among the various initiatives?

Monitoring the implementation and progress of all restoration activities and actions does not appear to be the objective of any one entity in this restoration initiative. The Gulf Coast Ecosystem Restoration Council is responsible for reporting on the progress of projects or programs to protect the Gulf Coast region under the Comprehensive Plan and State Plans, but appears to have limited authorities over other activities. This could lead to questions such as:

- Is the Council considered the over-arching entity for measuring the progress of restoration based on all restoration actions, or those just associated with the Comprehensive Plan? Does it have authorities that it is not using?

- Will the Council be measuring the progress of individual projects and programs or addressing the overall, holistic view of restoration?

- When the fund is empty and the Council is dissolved, who will be responsible for maintaining the restoration initiative or measuring its progress?

- Is adaptive management being contemplated by this restoration initiative to evaluate and guide restoration actions?

- Is there a process or entity that could change the direction of restoration efforts, and would they have the authority to initiate and carry out holistic changes or just changes to individual projects and programs?

Balancing Goals

Restoration in the Gulf Coast is different from some other restoration initiatives around the nation, primarily because a considerable amount of funding is expected to be provided up front toward the dual objectives of restoring the ecosystem and the economic vitality of the Gulf Coast. Some in Congress might wish to weigh on how efficiently funds are used to satisfy the dual goals of restoration and economic vitality, and may conduct oversight on balance of resources used for restoring the ecosystem versus restoring the economy of the region. Under the RESTORE Act and Treasury regulations, there are no formulas or provisions that address the exact balance of efforts to restore the ecosystem and the economy. Acknowledging that these two objectives are not mutually exclusive, preliminary questions could include:

---

[81] Under 33 U.S.C. 1321(t)(3)(B)(i) state plans are to take into consideration the Comprehensive Plan and be consistent with the goals and objectives of that plan.

- How will funding allocated from the Trust Fund address the dual goals of ecosystem restoration and economic restoration?

- Under state plans, will there be guidance on how funds should be split among economic and ecosystem-related projects?

- Is restoration funding derived from the Trust Fund intended to replace base state funding for ecosystem restoration and economic vitality or add to existing funding in state budgets?[82]

- The Comprehensive Plan contains seven objectives and notes that funding for these objectives will not be equally distributed.[83] How will the funding be distributed? Are the objectives prioritized?

- Is the Comprehensive Plan prioritizing ecological activities over economic activities?

- Will the concept of ecosystem services be used to determine the priority of projects to be implemented? If so, how will the assessment of ecosystem services be conducted?

Concluding Remarks

The restoration initiative in the Gulf Coast region is still in its infancy. Several aspects of its planning, implementation, and funding are uncertain or still being developed. However, recent developments, such as the promulgation of the U.S. Treasury Department regulations on the creation and allocation of funds from the Trust Fund, and the release of the initial Comprehensive Plan authorized under the RESTORE Act, have increased the attention on Gulf Coast restoration. As the multiple processes governing Gulf Coast restoration move forward, Congress might consider questions related to the coordination, planning, and implementation of these efforts, and may look to other comparable initiatives for lessons learned that could be incorporated into work on the Gulf Coast. Questions aimed at addressing adaptive management, governance, and striking a balance between restoration and the economy could be among the other issues raised in congressional oversight of Gulf Coast restoration.

---

[82] Under the Great Lakes Restoration Initiative (GLRI), federal funding for the initiative is provided largely in addition to existing, base funding for restoration actions. Federal agencies are specifically directed not to substitute GLRI funding for existing funding.

[83] *Initial Comprehensive Plan*, p. 11.

Appendix.

Table A-1. Sources of Funding for Restoration in the Gulf Region

(includes established and potential sources; does not include allocations for non-restoration activities)

Source/Mechanism	Status	Amount and Uses for Restoration Activities
BP criminal settlement	Approved by the U.S. District Court in the Eastern District of Louisiana on January 29, 2013	$2.394 billion to National Fish and Wildlife Foundation (NFWF) to support restoration efforts in the Gulf states related to the damages from the *Deepwater Horizon* oil spill. NFWF will allocate funding as follows: -50% to support barrier island and/or river projects in Louisiana -14% to support projects Alabama -14% to support projects Florida -14% to support projects Mississippi -8% to support projects in Texas $100 million to the North American Wetlands Conservation Fund for the "purpose of wetlands restoration and conservation projects" in the Gulf states or "otherwise designed to benefit migratory bird species and other wildlife affected by the [*Deepwater Horizon*] oil spill."
Transocean Civil Settlement	Announced January 3, 2013; subject to court approval	$1 billion, of which 20% goes to the Oil Spill Liability Trust Fund and 80% ($800 million) goes into the Gulf Coast Restoration Trust Fund, to be divided as outlined under the RESTORE Act (P.L. 112-141, see "RESTORE Act Funding" Section): -35% divided equally among the five Gulf states to be applied toward one or more of 11 designated activities (including environmental and economic objectives); -30% disbursed by the Council to the five Gulf states, based on specific criteria (i.e. not equal shares): shoreline impact, oiled shoreline distance from the Deepwater Horizon rig, and coastal population. Each state must submit a plan for approval, documenting how funding will support one or more of the 11 designated activities;

Source/Mechanism	Status	Amount and Uses for Restoration Activities
		-30% provided to a newly created Gulf Coast Ecosystem Restoration Council to finance ecosystem restoration activities in the Gulf Coast region; and
		-2.5% for the Gulf Coast Ecosystem Restoration Science, Observation, Monitoring, and Technology Program;
		-2.5% to the five Gulf states to establish "centers of excellence" through a competitive grant program.
Transocean criminal settlement	Announced January 3, 2013; subject to court approval	$150 million to NFWF to support restoration efforts in the Gulf states related to the damages from the *Deepwater Horizon* oil spill. NFWF will allocate funding as follows: -50% to support barrier island and/or river projects in Louisiana -14% to support projects in Alabama -14% to support projects in Florida -14% to support projects in Mississippi -8% to support projects in in Texas
MOEX civil settlement	Approved by the U.S. District Court in the Eastern District of Louisiana on June 8, 2012	$25 million is to be distributed in various amounts among the five Gulf states for unspecified purposes Supplement environmental projects: -Florida ($5 million); -Louisiana ($6.75 million); -Mississippi ($5 million); and -Texas ($3.25 million)

Source: Table compiled by CRS.

Table A-2. Federal Ecosystem Restoration in the Gulf

(selected federal coordination and funding efforts in the Gulf Coast region)

Initiative	Description/Issue Addressed	Agency Lead
Louisiana Coastal Area Protection and Restoration Plan (LCAPR)	Comprehensive ecosystem restoration and hurricane protection plan for Coastal Louisiana.	Corps
Louisiana Coastal Area Near-Term Plan (LCA)	Projects to improve ecosystem function in coastal Louisiana, as well as other incidental benefits. Projects include beneficial use of dredged material, diversion of sediment and water, barrier island restoration, and coastal protection	Corps
Mississippi Area Coastal Improvement Program (MsCIP)	Comprehensive planning to address hurricane/storm damage reduction, salt water intrusion, shoreline erosion, fish and wildlife preservation through restoration and flood control projects in coastal Mississippi.	Corps
Gulf Hypoxia Task Force	Provides executive level direction and support for coordinating the actions of ten states and five federal agencies working on nutrient management within the Mississippi River and Gulf of Mexico watershed.	EPA (Chair)
Comprehensive Everglades Restoration Plan (CERP)	Federal/state framework to restore, protect, and preserve the water resources of central and southern Florida, including the Everglades.	Corps/DOI
National Ocean Council	Coordinates federal stewardship efforts for oceans through support for regional planning bodies, including one such body for the Gulf of Mexico.	CEQ/OSTP (Co-Chairs)
National Estuary Program (NEP)	Works to restore and maintain water quality and ecological integrity of estuaries of national significance. Seven of 18 NEPs are in the Gulf Region.	EPA
Gulf of Mexico Program/Gulf of Mexico Alliance	Program to facilitate collaborative actions to protect, maintain, and restore health and productivity of the Gulf of Mexico. Made up of Gulf Coast governors and supported by thirteen federal agencies.	EPA (DOI, NOAA co-leads)
Coastal Wetlands Planning Protection and Restoration Act (CWPPRA)	Federal/state program which focuses on marsh creation, restoration, protection, and enhancement as well as barrier island restoration. CWPPRA has planned and designed several larger-scale projects which may be constructed by other initiatives.	FWS
Coastal Impact Assistance Program (CIAP)	Provides grants to coastal oil and gas producing states from Outer Continental Shelf revenues. Funding goes toward coastal restoration and infrastructure to mitigate activities arising from mineral exploration.	MMS
Coastal and Estuarine Land Conservation Program (CELCP)	Provides matching funds to state and local governments to purchase significant coastal and estuarine lands from willing sellers.	NOAA
North American Wetlands Conservation Act (NAWCA)	Provides matching grants to organizations and individuals who have developed partnerships to carry out wetlands conservation projects for the benefit of wetlands-associated migratory birds and other wildlife.	FWS

Source: Table compiled by CRS from multiple sources including *Gulf of Mexico Regional Ecosystem Restoration Strategy* and *America's Gulf Coast: A Long-Term Recovery Plan after the Deepwater Horizon Oil Spill* (also referred to as the "Mabus Report").

Notes: List is illustrative of federal efforts only and does not include state-led efforts. List of federal efforts is not exhaustive. "CEQ" indicates White House Council on Environmental Quality; "OSTP" indicates White House Office of Science and Technology Policy.

Author Contact Information

Charles V. Stern
Specialist in Natural Resources Policy
cstern@crs.loc.gov, 7-7786

Pervaze A. Sheikh
Specialist in Natural Resources Policy
psheikh@crs.loc.gov, 7-6070

Jonathan L. Ramseur
Specialist in Environmental Policy
jramseur@crs.loc.gov, 7-7919